Instant Bulletin Boards

Month by Month Classroom Graphics

Anthony Flores

Makemaster® Blackline Masters

Fearon Teacher Aids, Carthage, Illinois

I would like to dedicate this book to my loving parents, Manuel and Mary Flores.

Development and Production editor: Gustavo Medina
Designer: Joe di Chiarro
Cover designer: Joe di Chiarro
Illustrators: Anthony Flores, and Anne Jaekel
Design manager: Susan True

ISBN-0-8224-3900-X
Printed in the United States of America
1. 19 18 17 16 15 14

Contents

Introduction

Bulletin boards traditionally have been a part of the elementary school classroom. Whether to relay information, help keep track of days and holidays, call attention to special awards and events, or simply create an interesting and decorative area in the classroom, bulletin boards are an important part of the classroom environment.

Instant Bulletin Boards features quick and easy methods for preparing bulletin board borders, lettering, figures, calendars and calendar keepers, and border sheets. Border sheets are blank sheets with decorative borders that add visual appeal and interest to lessons, handouts, tests, or quizzes and are designed to complement the monthly bulletin boards.

The first part of the book shows step-by-step constructions for these different bulletin board components. The second part of the book includes a section for each month of the school year. Each of these sections contains a variety of borders, lettering, figures, calendar keepers, and border sheets that relate thematically to the month. You and your students can combine these elements in any number of ways to make the bulletin board uniquely yours. Or you can simply repeat the bulletin boards shown on the Instant Month pages if your time is in short supply.

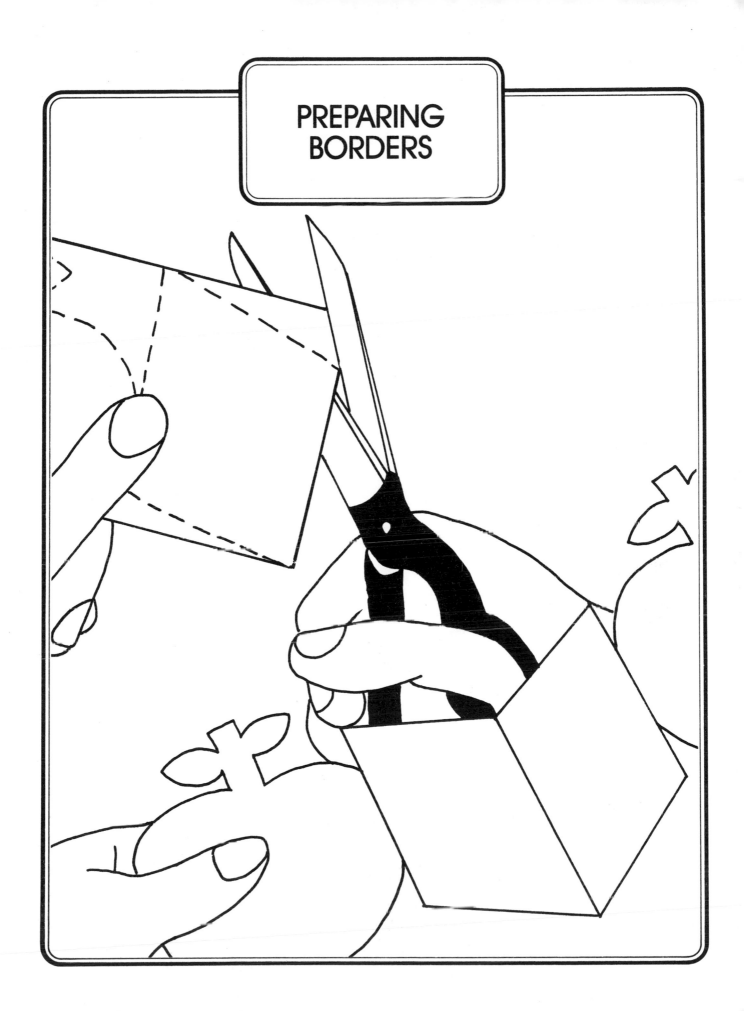

PREPARING
BORDERS

A Step-by-Step Guide to Preparing Borders

Step **1**   Choose one of the border patterns for the month. We have chosen one of the September borders for this guide.

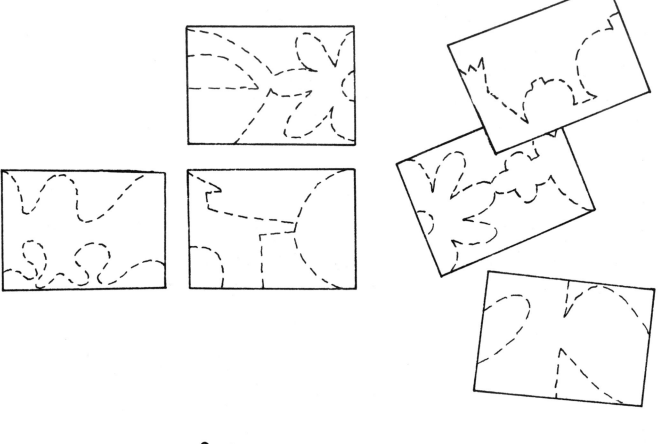

Step **2**   Choose construction paper in the color you wish to use for your border. Cut the construction paper into strips 18 inches long and 3 inches wide. Cut as many strips as you will need to enclose your bulletin board.

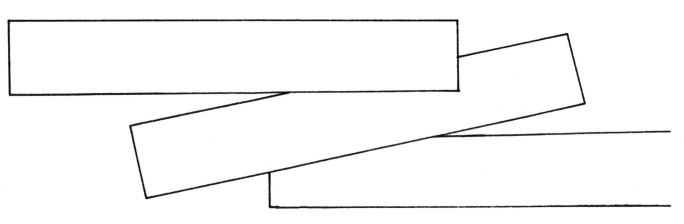

Step **3** **a.** Fold a strip in half.

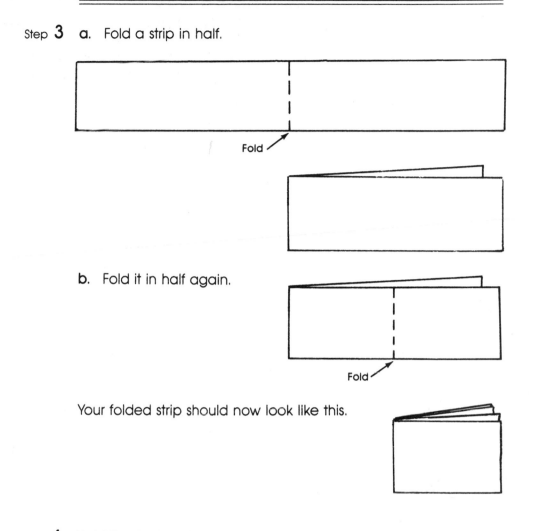

b. Fold it in half again.

Your folded strip should now look like this.

Step **4** Hold the folded strip in the center and cut it using one of the following methods. Try each of the methods to find the one that works best for you.

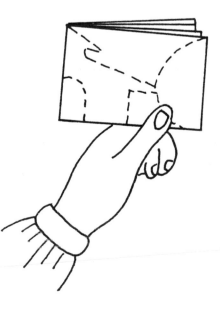

a. Cut the strip freehand.
b. Draw the design on the strip freehand, then cut it out.
c. Trace the design on lightweight paper and cut it out to form a template. Then place the template on the folded strip and cut around the template.

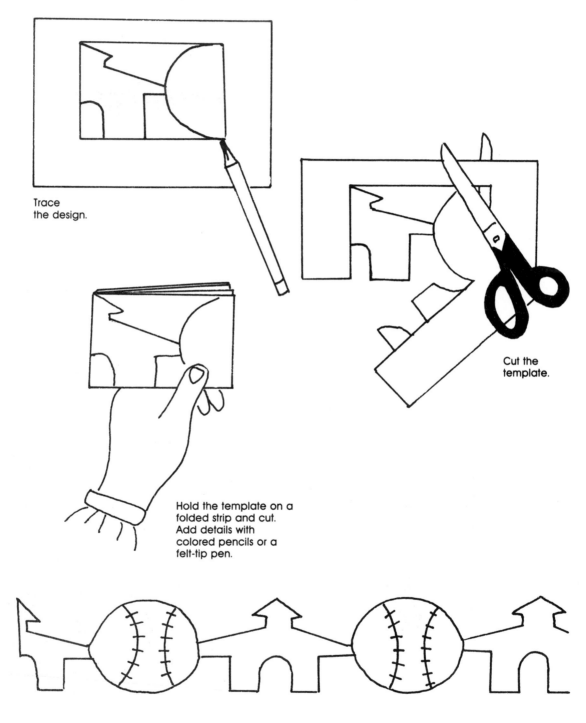

Trace
the design.

Cut the
template.

Hold the template on a
folded strip and cut.
Add details with
colored pencils or a
felt-tip pen.

d. Use carbon paper to transfer the design to thin cardboard. Cut out the pattern around the cardboard to form a template. Place the cardboard template on the folded strip, trace around it with a pencil and cut along the lines you have drawn.

Remember to cut as many strips as you need to complete your border.

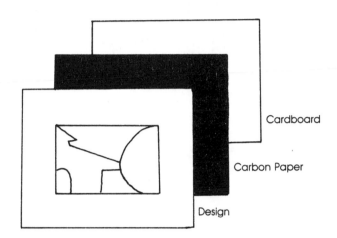

Cardboard

Carbon Paper

Design

Step **5** Staple or pin the border strips around your bulletin board.

Now you are ready to make any of the borders shown in this book. Once you are familiar with the technique, you can create your own patterns. You can also place borders one inside the other to make double borders.

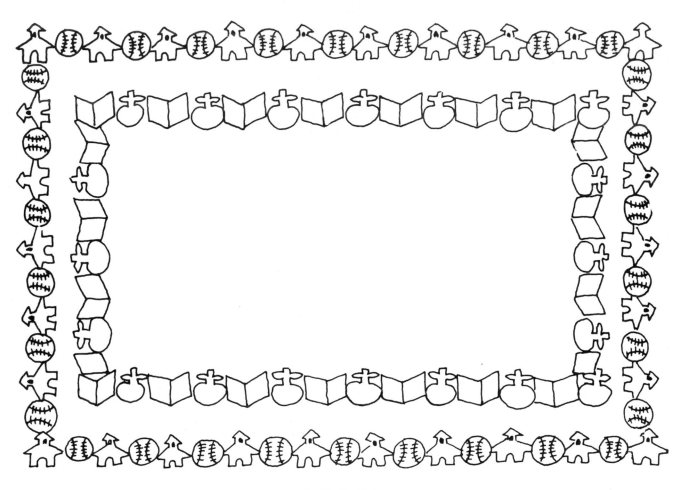

Double Borders

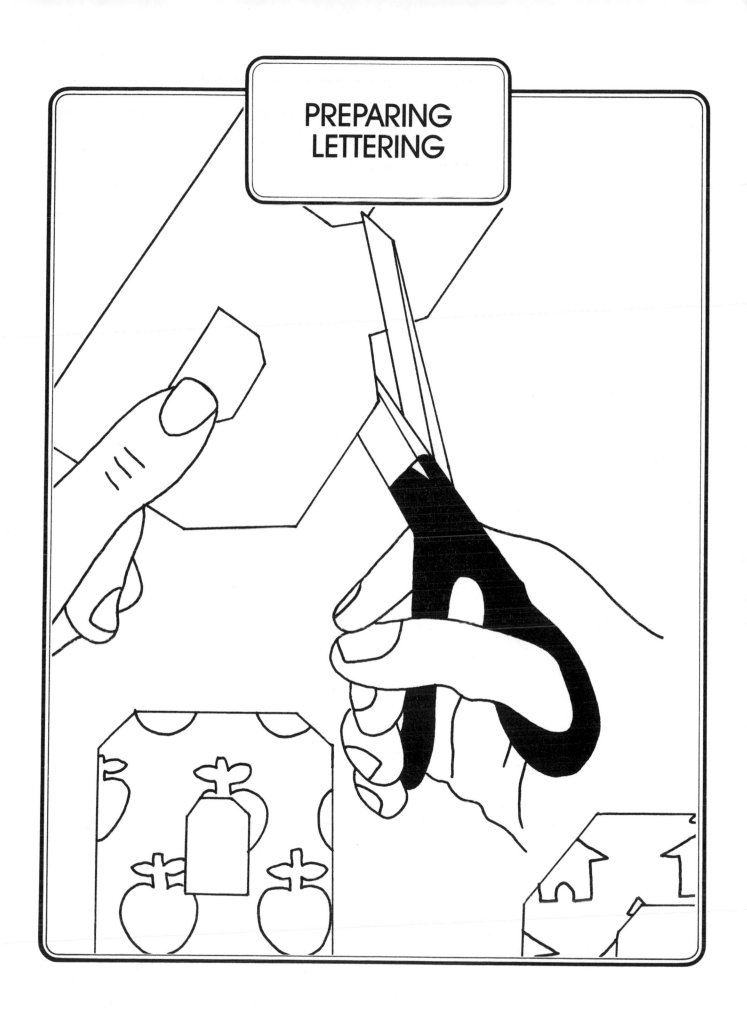

PREPARING
LETTERING

A Step-by-Step Guide to Preparing Lettering

Step **1**   Use tagboard and the guide letters in the Letters Appendix to make a set of letters.

Cut the letters out. They will be used for tracing purposes.

Step **2**   Use a lettering pattern sheet of repeated figures from one of the monthly sections to make a ditto master. This may be done in either of two ways:

a.   Run the pattern page through a copying machine that makes ditto masters.

or

b. Lay the lettering pattern sheet over a regular ditto master and firmly trace over figures with a ballpoint pen.

Step 3 To add color to your figures and letters:

a. Run dittos on white ditto paper. Have students outline figures in crayon or felt-tip pen and color them in.

or

b. Run dittos on colored ditto paper and draw the figure outlines only.

or

c. Run one sheet of colored construction paper at a time through the ditto machine and draw the figure outlines.

Remember to prepare as many letters and sheets as you will need for the message you will be cutting out.

Step **4** Lay cut-out letters on completed pattern sheets. Outline the letters in pencil and cut them out.

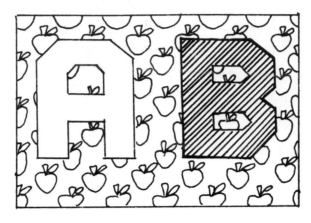

Instant Backgrounds Instead of making dittos, use:

a. Wallpaper

b. Newspaper

c. Wrapping paper

d. Contact paper

e. Plain construction paper

f. Pages from magazines and comic books

g. Pages from catalogs

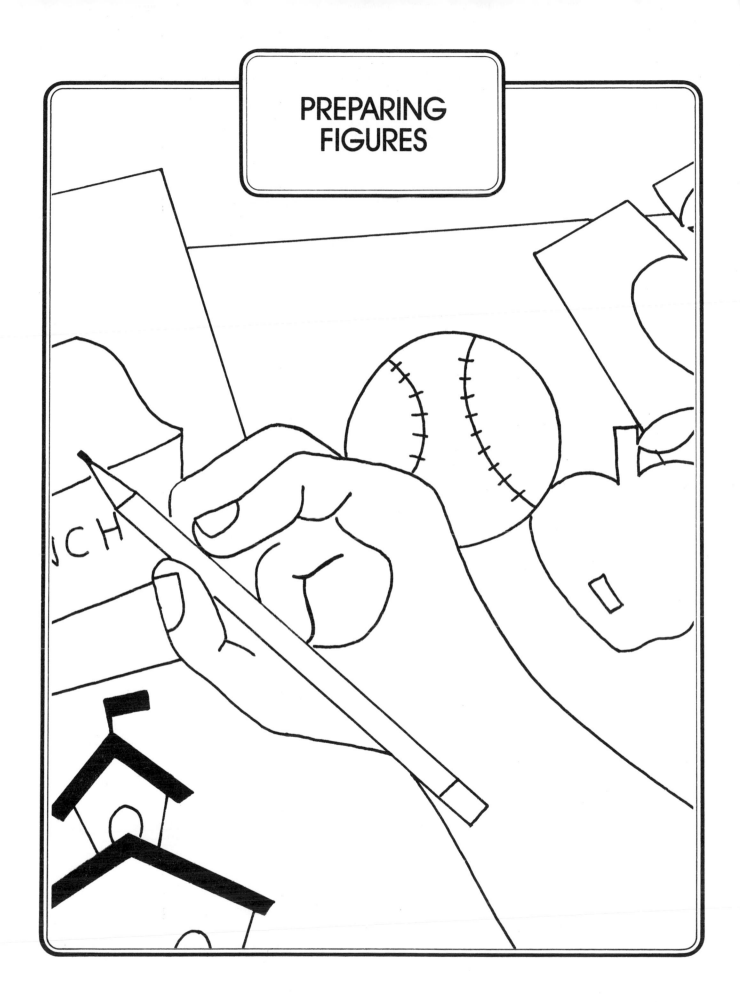

PREPARING
FIGURES

Step-by-Step Methods of Preparing Figures

Use the method below that works best for you.

Opaque Projector

Step **1** Place the pattern in the projector and focus it on paper that has been tacked or taped to the wall.

Step **2** Trace the figure outlines in pencil, then use one of the finishing methods listed on page 16.

Step **3** Cut the figures from the paper and use them on a bulletin board.

Hand-Drawn Transparencies

Step **1** Trace the pattern onto an acetate transparency film using a felt-tip pen made for this purpose.

Step **2** Place the transparency in the overhead projector and project the image onto paper that has been tacked or taped to the wall.

Step **3** Trace the figure outlines in pencil, then use one of the finishing methods listed on page 16.

Step **4** Cut the figures from the paper and use them on a bulletin board.

Freehand Drawing

Step **1** Copy the pattern by sketching it in pencil.

Step **2** Finish it using one of the methods described on page 16.

Step **3** Cut the figures from the paper and use them on a bulletin board.

Methods of Finishing Figures

a. Paint figures with tempera or watercolors and outline them with black felt-tip pens.

b. Color figures with colored felt-tip pens.

c. Color figures with crayons.

d. Combine painted areas with yarn-filled areas, fabric-filled areas, and areas filled in with white glue and glitter.

e. Outline figures in felt-tip pen and fill them in with crushed tissue or with flat tissue applied with liquid starch.

PREPARING CALENDARS AND CALENDAR KEEPERS

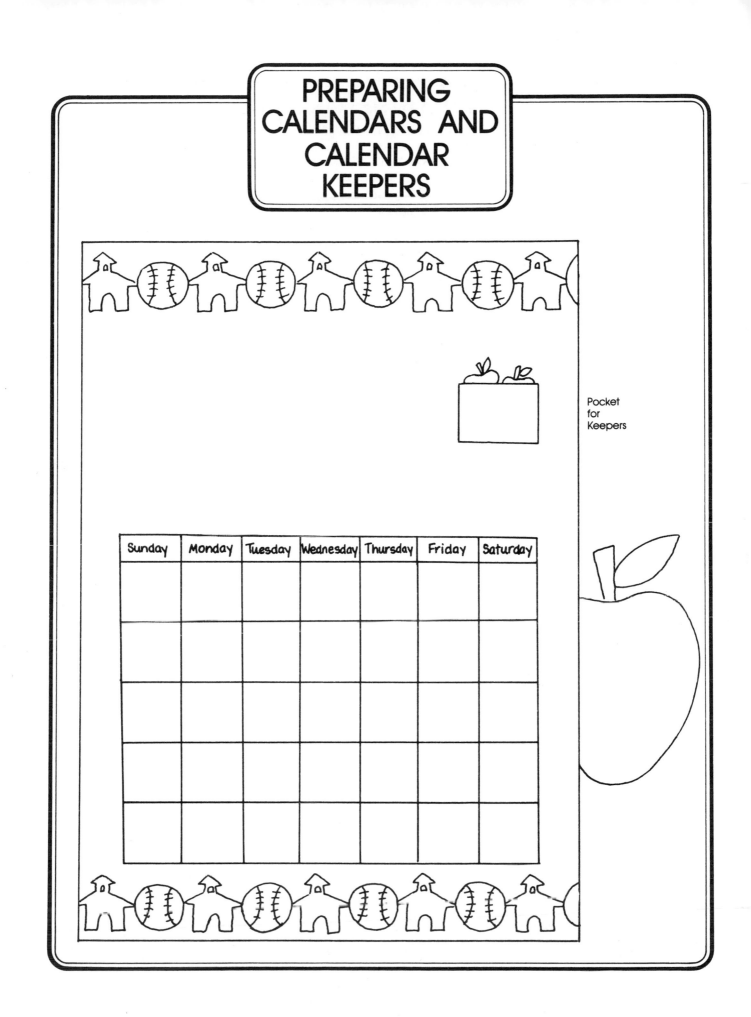

Pocket for Keepers

Sunday	Monday	Tuesday	Wednesday	Thursday	Friday	Saturday

A Step-by-Step Guide to Preparing the Calendar and the Calendar Keepers

Calendar keepers are used on the blank calendar to keep track of days, special events, and so forth. Each day a new calendar keeper is stapled or glued to the appropriate square on the calendar.

Step **1** Place a calendar keeper pattern on top of heavy paper or tagboard. Trace its outline.

Step **2** Cut out the pattern outline to form a template.

Step **3** Trace around the template on colored construction paper. Cut as many objects as you will need for a particular month—for example, make 30 apples for September. (You may want to use a different shape of calendar keeper to mark special days and occasions.)

Step **4**   Finish the keepers using one of the methods of finishing figures listed on page 16.

Step **5**   Glue on or draw desired details.

Step **6**   Use a felt-tip pen to number or label each keeper.

Step **7**   Use the opaque projector or freehand method (see Preparing Figures) to duplicate the calendar pattern on page 20.

Step **8**   Put together a border pattern, the calendar pattern, and the calendar keepers, and you have a calendar board! Remember that you can use different calendar keepers to indicate special dates or events.

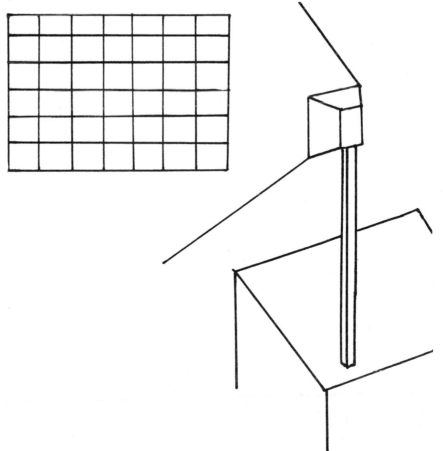

Enlarge to 3½- or 4-inch squares.

Year-round Calendar Pattern

Sunday	Monday	Tuesday	Wednesday	Thursday	Friday	Saturday

PREPARING
BORDER SHEETS

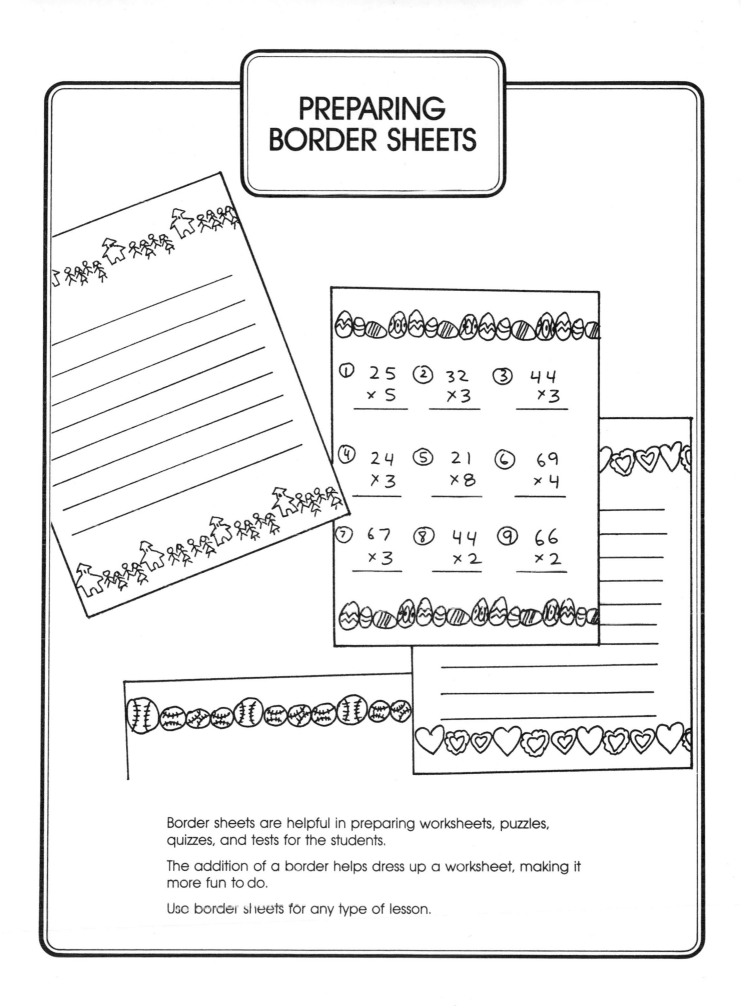

① 25 ② 32 ③ 44
   ×5   ×3   ×3

④ 24 ⑤ 21 ⑥ 69
   ×3   ×8   ×4

⑦ 67 ⑧ 44 ⑨ 66
   ×3   ×2   ×2

Border sheets are helpful in preparing worksheets, puzzles, quizzes, and tests for the students.

The addition of a border helps dress up a worksheet, making it more fun to do.

Use border sheets for any type of lesson.

Methods of Preparing Border Sheets

Thermafax Method

Make a worksheet using a border sheet page from this book and thermafax it. Here, however, the border would be used only once.

Copier Method

Use a copying machine to make as many copies of the worksheet as you need.

Ditto Master Method

Place a border sheet from this book on a ditto master. Firmly trace over the design with a ballpoint pen. Then type or print the lesson of your choice on the master.

Carbon part
of ditto master

INSTANT
MONTHS

September Borders

Add lines to show the folds in the books and to separate the books from the apples. Add titles to the books.

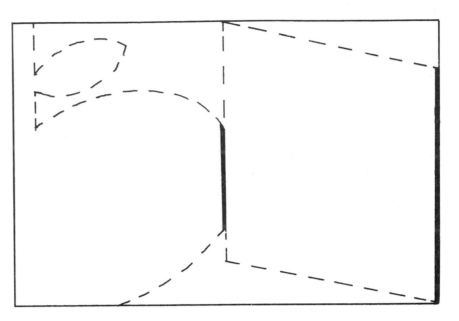

APPLES AND BOOKS

FOOTBALLS AND NOTEBOOKS

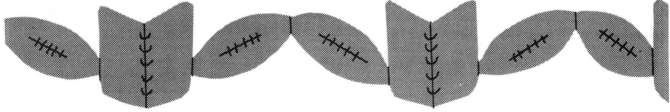

Add lines to separate the notebooks from the footballs. Cut out laces and paste them on the footballs, or draw them in. Add rings to the notebooks.

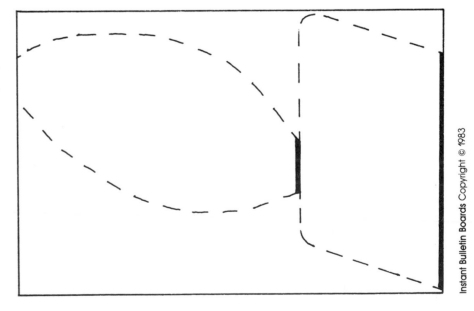

Draw lines on the balls.

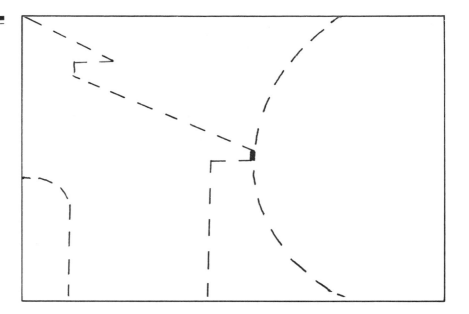

SCHOOLHOUSES AND BALLS

NOTEBOOKS AND LEAVES

Add lines to show rings and folds in books.

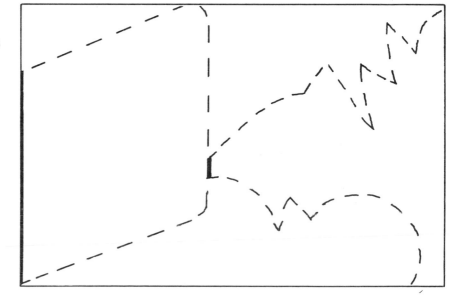

September Figures

September Calendar Keepers

RED APPLE

RED SCHOOLHOUSE

BROWN BALL

(Add lines with a felt-tip pen.)

ORANGE AND BROWN LEAVES

Instant October

October Borders

Add eyes and mouths with a felt-tip pen.

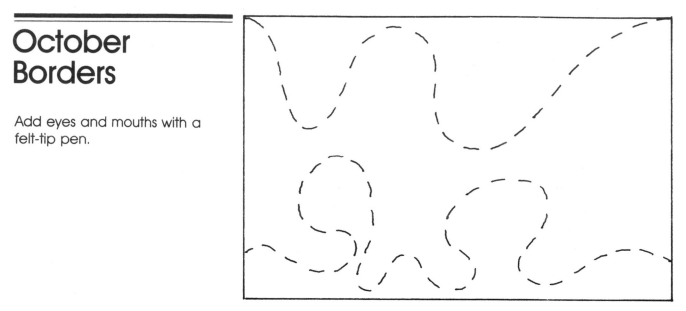

HAPPY GHOSTS

JACK-O'-LANTERNS AND HAYSTACKS

Draw in lines to separate the figures. Add faces to the pumpkins. Cut white ghost separately and glue to the back of haystacks.

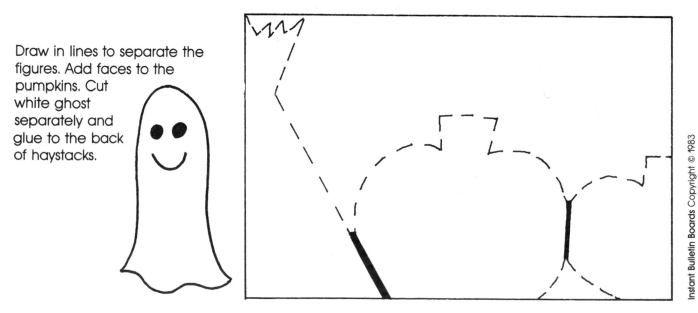

Cut and paste features on the large pumpkins. Draw in lines between pumpkins.

PUMPKINS AND JACK-O'-LANTERNS

PUMPKIN PATCH

Overlap this border with the pumpkin and jack-o'-lantern border to create a pumpkin patch.

October Figures

October Calendar Keepers

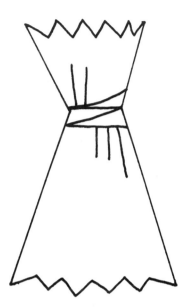

YELLOW CORNSTALK

ORANGE PUMPKIN

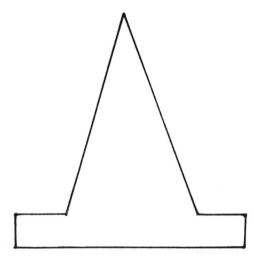

BLACK HAT

(Use white numbers to indicate days.)

GHOST

Instant Bulletin Boards Copyright © 1983

Instant November

November Borders

Add lines to gourds and pumpkins. Use the pattern to cut out turkey heads. Add eyes and lines on beaks. Glue heads to bodies.

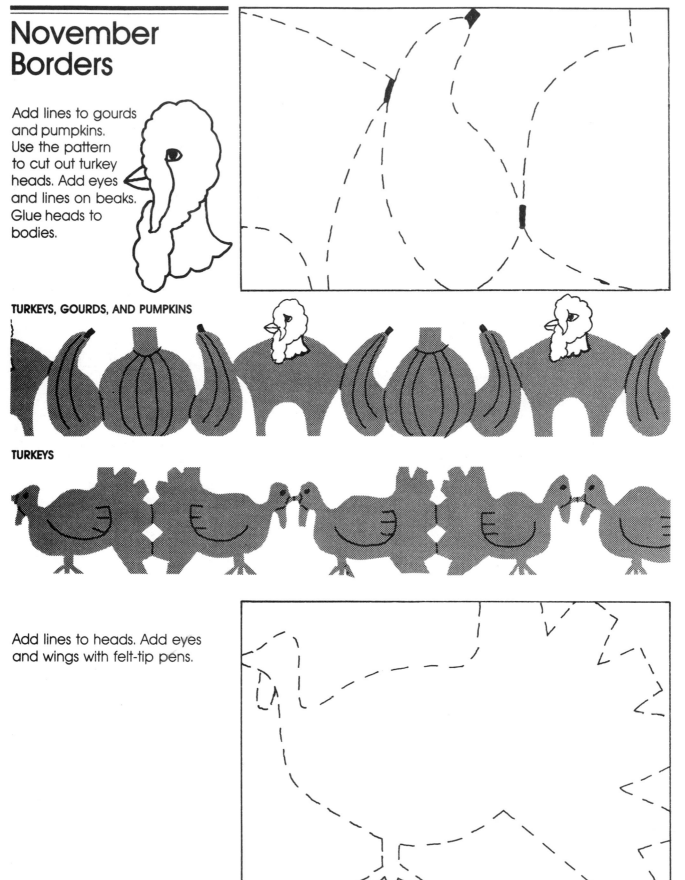

TURKEYS, GOURDS, AND PUMPKINS

TURKEYS

Add lines to heads. Add eyes and wings with felt-tip pens.

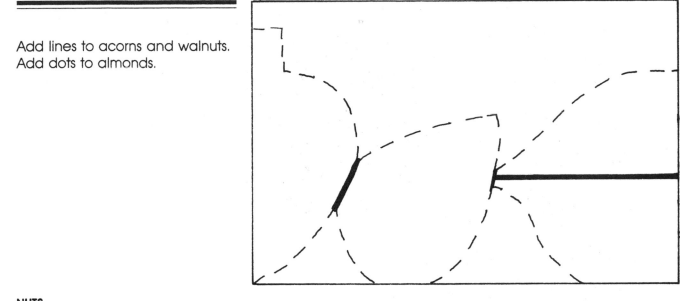

Add lines to acorns and walnuts.
Add dots to almonds.

NUTS

CORNSTALKS AND PUMPKINS

Add lines of varying thicknesses
to cornstalks and pumpkins.

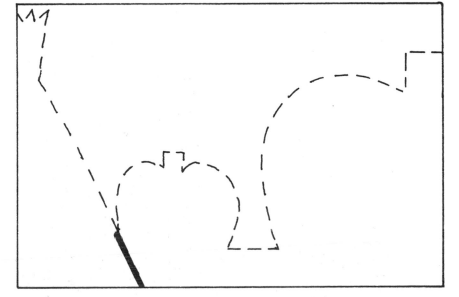

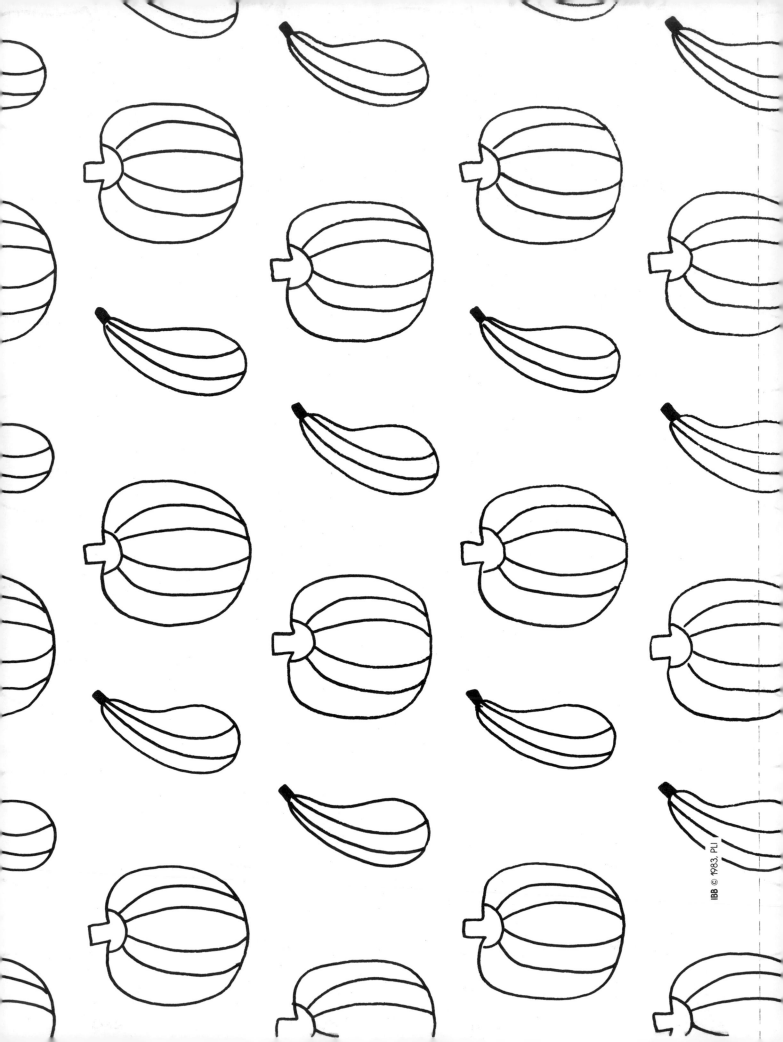

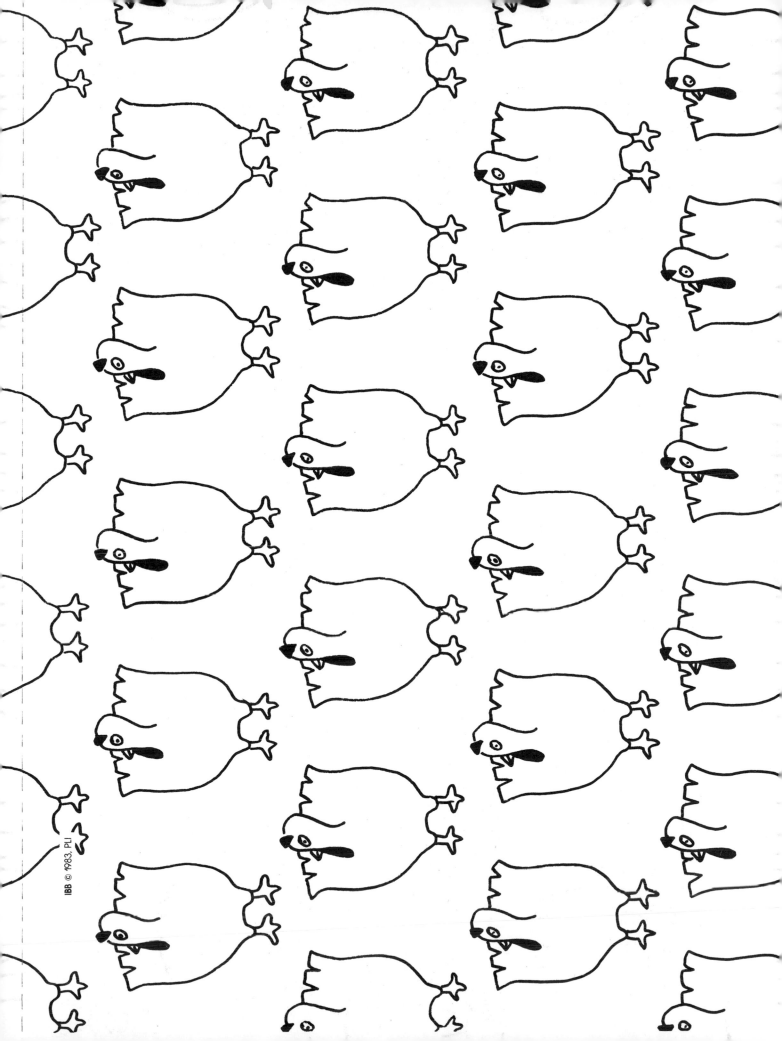

November Figures

November Calendar Keepers

BROWN TURKEY

ORANGE GOURD AND PUMPKIN

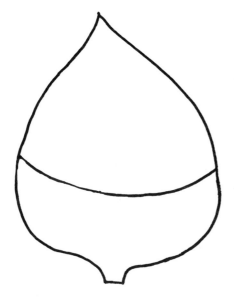

BROWN ACORN

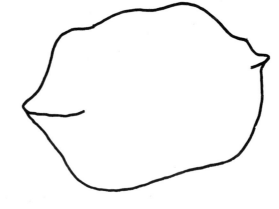

BROWN WALNUT

Instant December

December Borders

Add lines to separate figures.
Add decorations to ornaments.

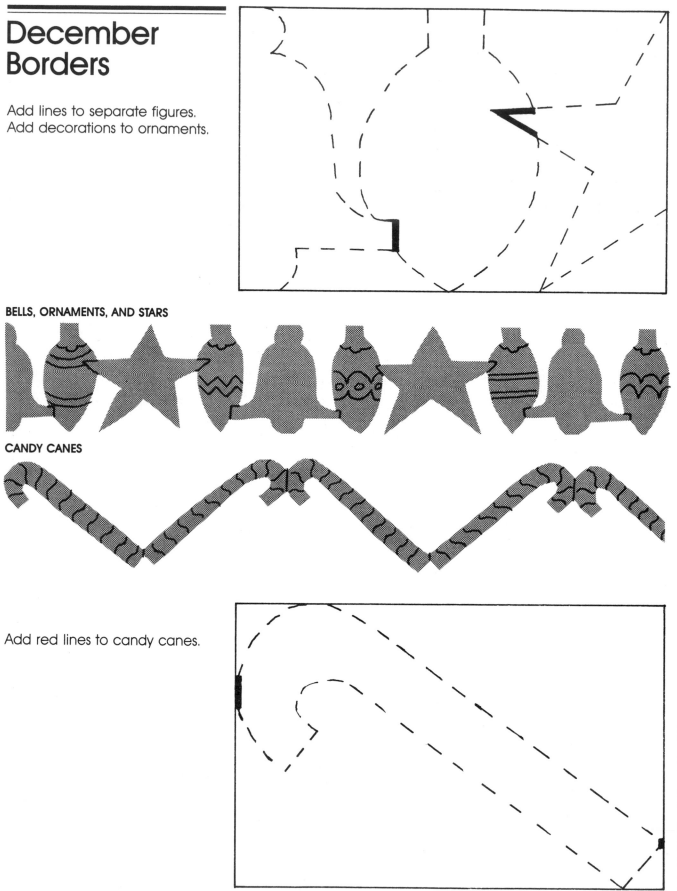

BELLS, ORNAMENTS, AND STARS

CANDY CANES

Add red lines to candy canes.

Add lines to separate trains and tops. Add designs to tops.

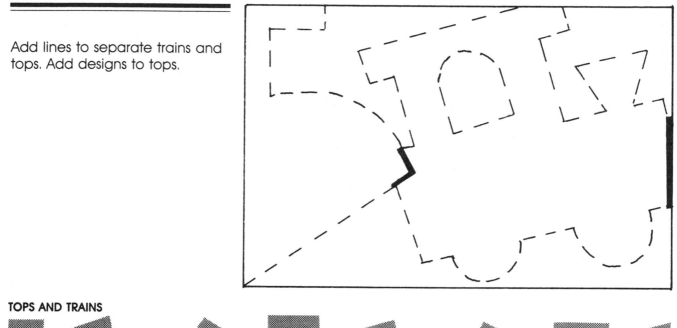

TOPS AND TRAINS

MENORAHS

Cut out yellow or gold flame and add to menorah.

December Figures

December Calendar Keepers

RED SLEIGH

GOLD MENORAH

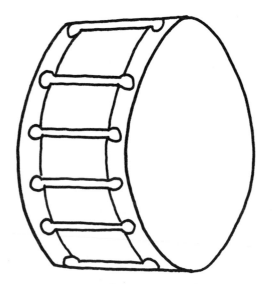

WHITE DRUM

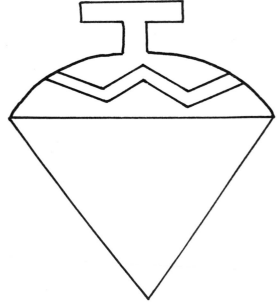

YELLOW TOP

Instant January

January Borders

Add line to separate snowman and mountain. Add features and gloves and hats to snowmen.

SNOWMAN AND MOUNTAIN

DATE BORDER

Add the year to each section. Color in a border of scallops or add your own design.

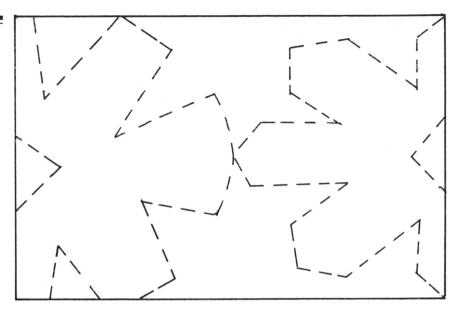

SNOWFLAKES

PENGUINS

Paint in beaks or add orange-
yellow pieces for beaks. Add
black lines to them. Add white
paper for chests.

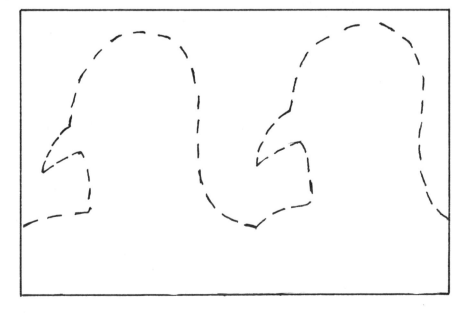

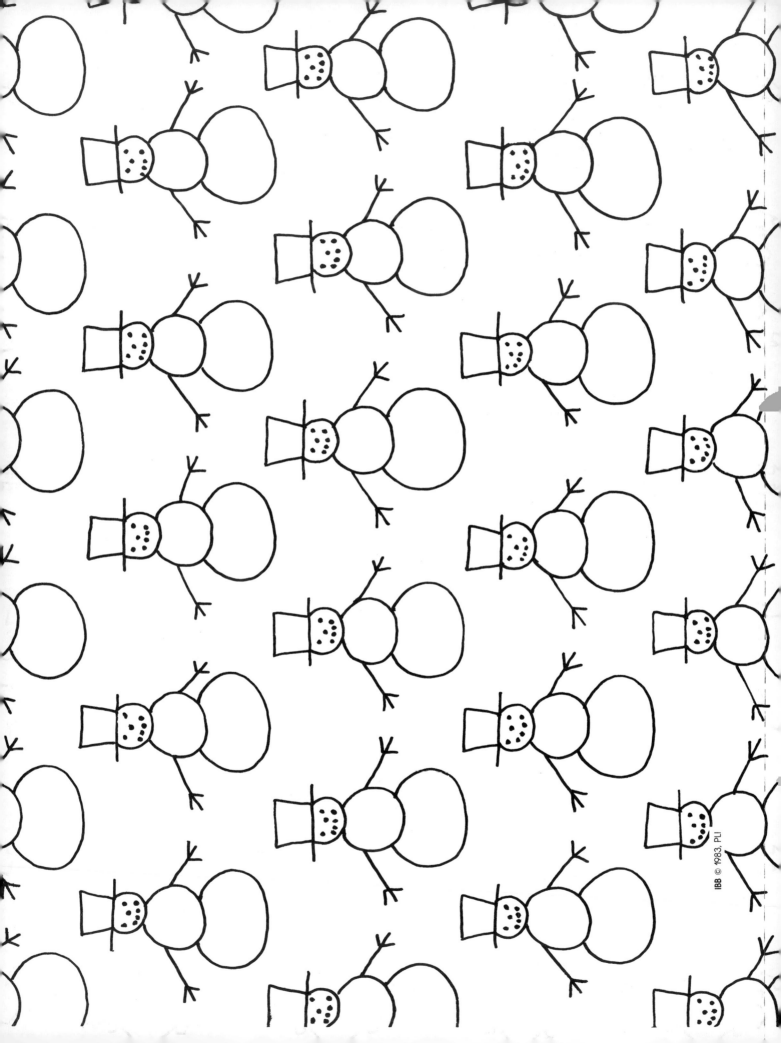

January Figures

January Calendar Keepers

TOP HAT

PENGUIN

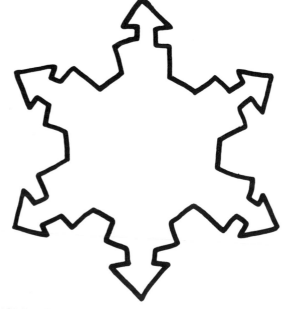

SNOWFLAKE

NEW YEAR'S HAT AND WHISTLE

Instant February

February Borders

Add lines between hearts and scissors. Add messages to large hearts.

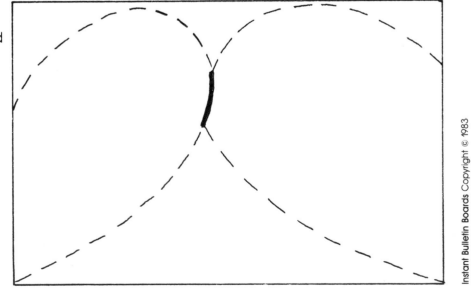

SCISSORS AND HEARTS

I Love You

So Sweet

VALENTINES

ove
u

Be Mine

Mine

Love

MY VALENTINE

F

Add lines to separate hearts. Add messages with felt-tip pens.

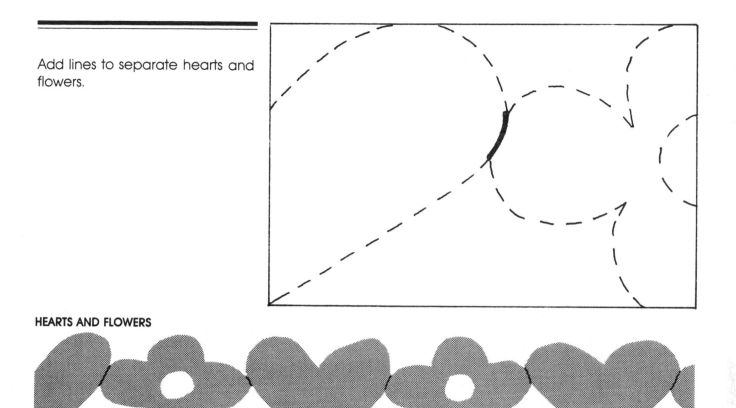

Add lines to separate hearts and flowers.

HEARTS AND FLOWERS

INSIDE-OUTSIDE HEARTS

Add lines between "outside" hearts and rectangles.

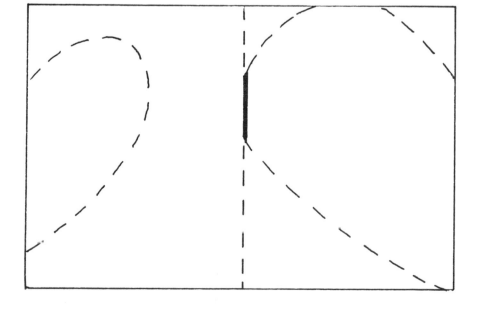

February Figures

February Calendar Keepers

RED HEART

WHITE HEART WITH TRIM

RED CUPID

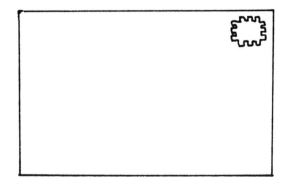

WHITE ENVELOPE

LOVE♡LOVE♡LOVE♡LOVE♡

LOVE♡LOVE♡LOVE♡LOVE♡

Instant March

March Borders

Draw designs on butterfly wings. Add eyes and lines to separate butterflies.

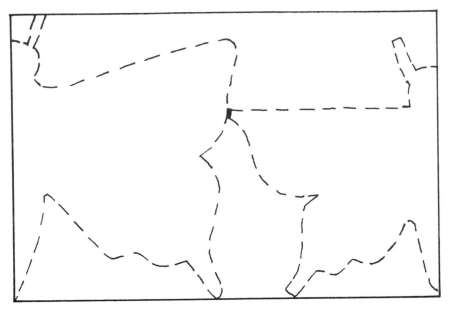

BUTTERFLIES

FLOWERS, FLOWERS, FLOWERS

Add lines to separate flowers. Add cut-and-paste centers to small flowers.

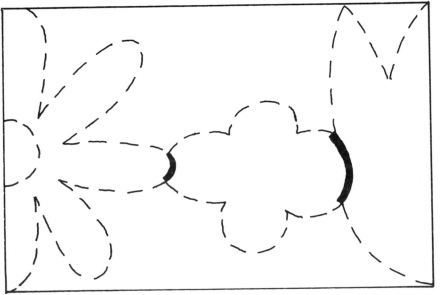

Instant Bulletin Boards Copyright © 1983

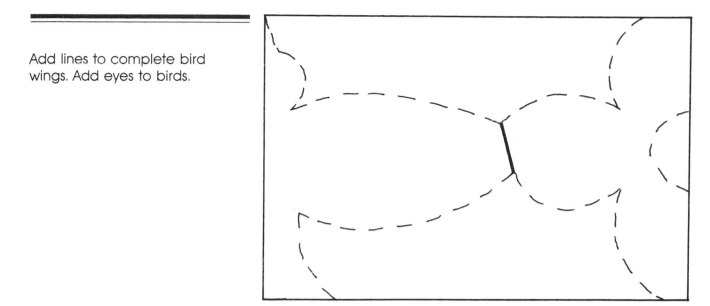

Add lines to complete bird wings. Add eyes to birds.

BIRDS AND FLOWERS

LADYBUGS

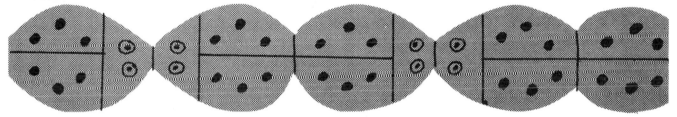

Add cut-and-paste dots for eyes and spots. Add lines for wings.

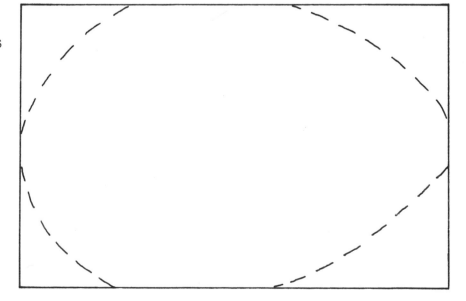

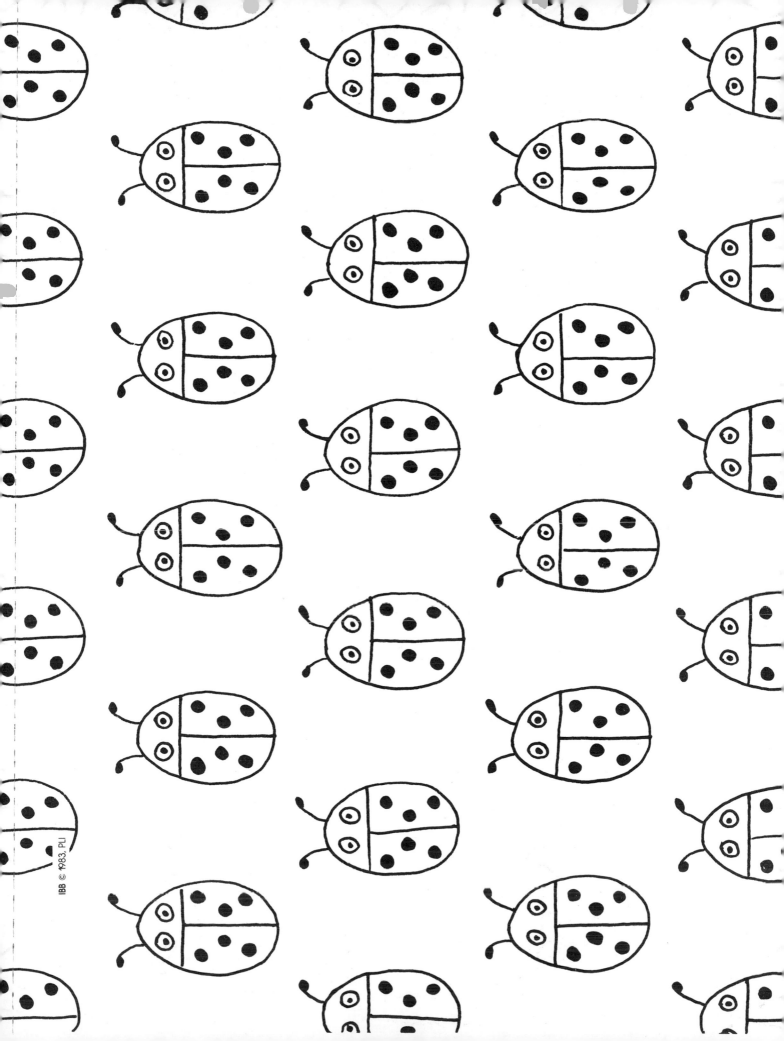

March Figures

March Calendar Keepers

BLUEBIRD

FLOWER

GREEN FROG

BUTTERFLY

Instant April

April Borders

Add eyes and noses.

RABBITS

DUCKS

Add eyes.

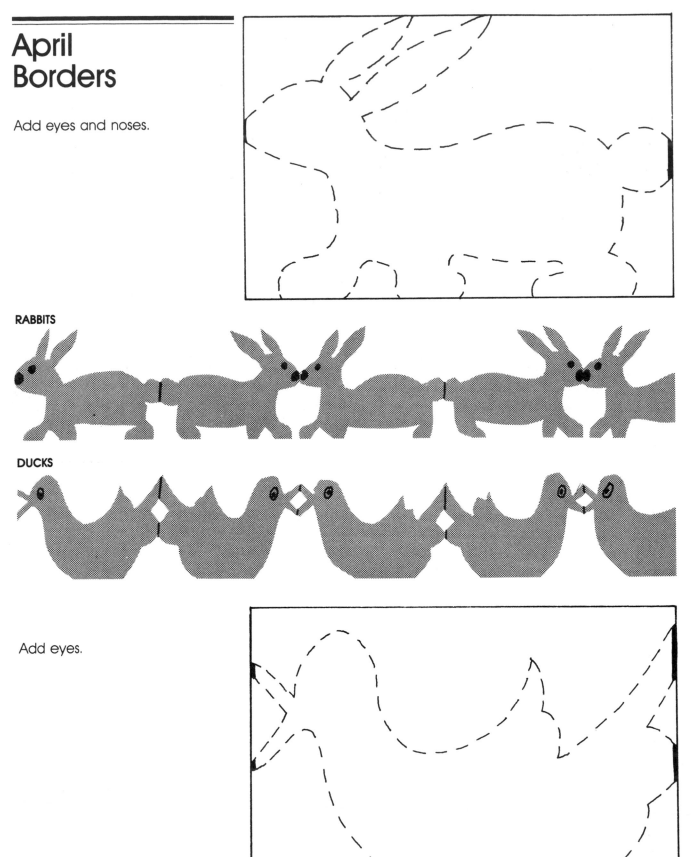

Add lines to separate eggs. Let children decorate the eggs with crayons or felt-tip pens.

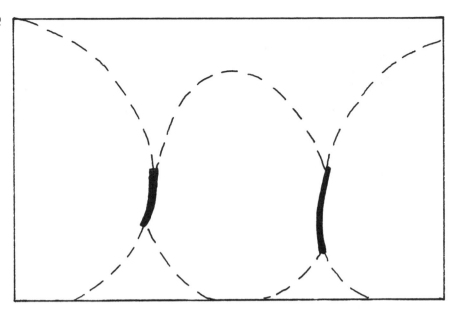

EASTER EGGS AND GRASS

Overlap grass border and Easter egg border.

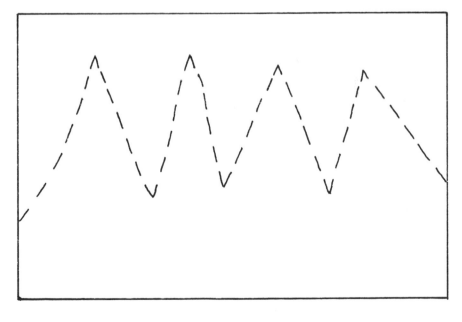

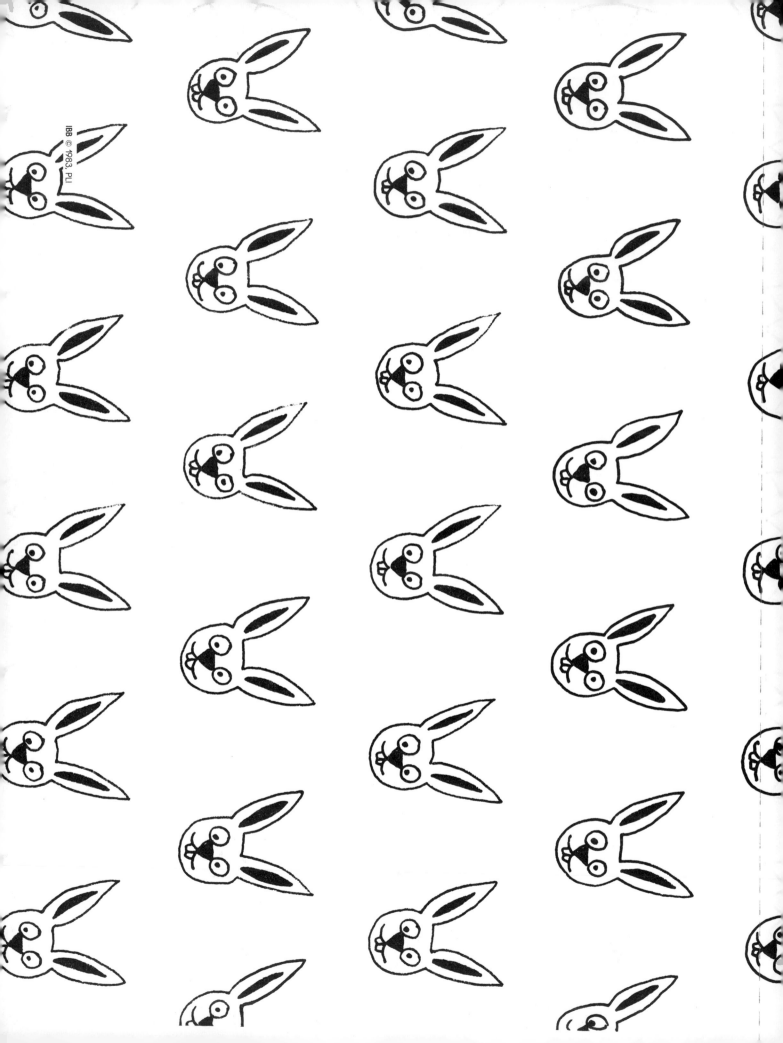

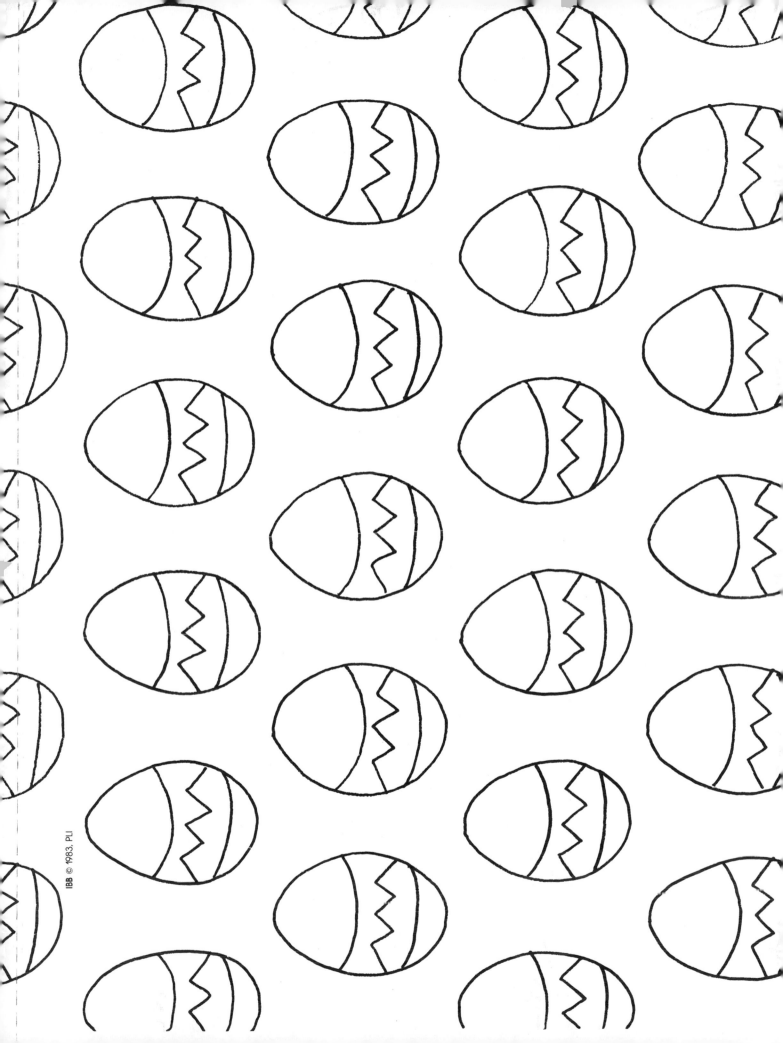

April Figures

April Calendar Keepers

DECORATED EGGS

YELLOW DUCK

CHICKEN

EGG BASKET

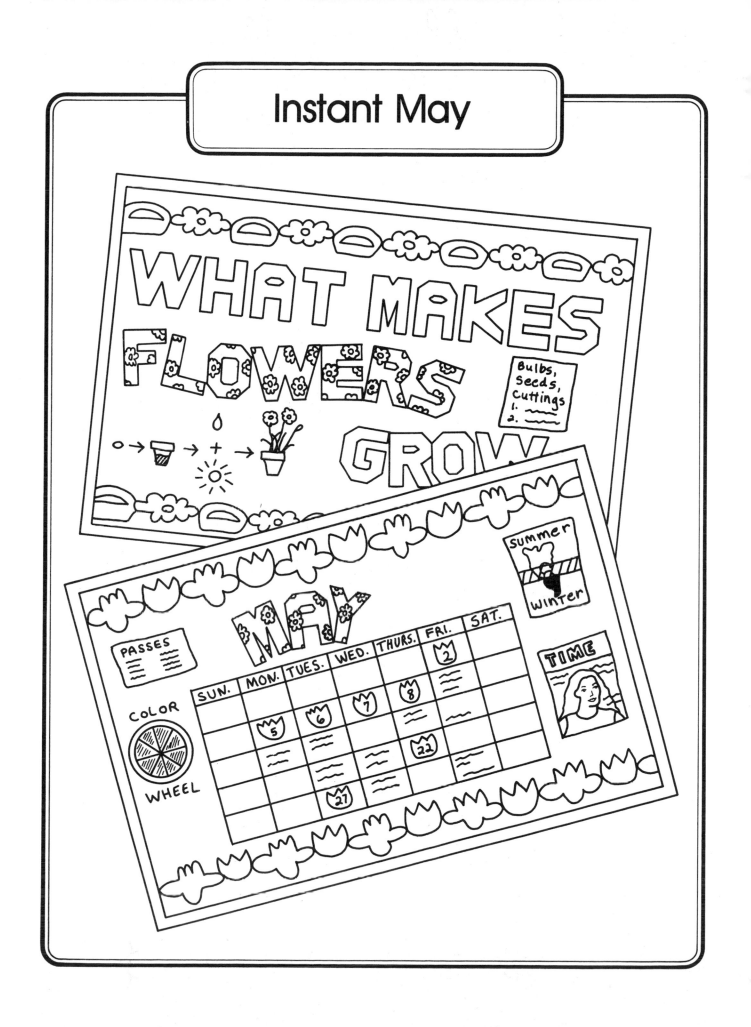

May Borders

Pattern for hot dog. Cut out of brown paper and paste behind hot dog bun.

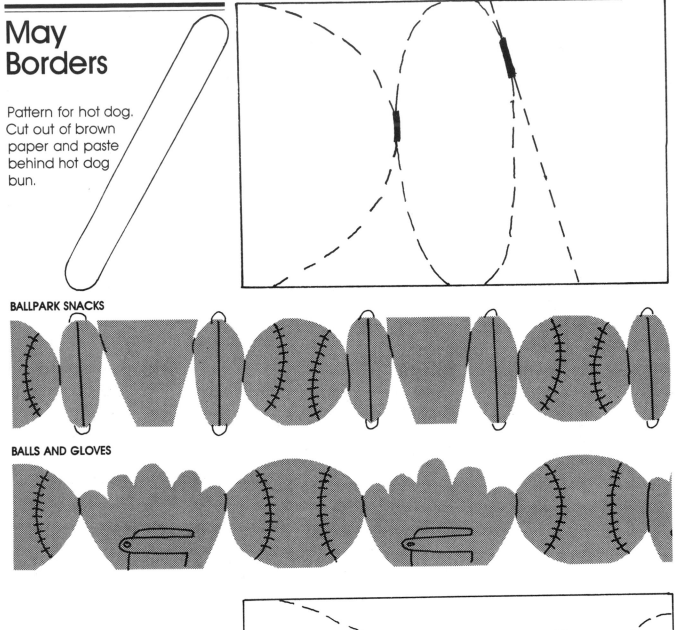

BALLPARK SNACKS

BALLS AND GLOVES

Add lines to balls and gloves.

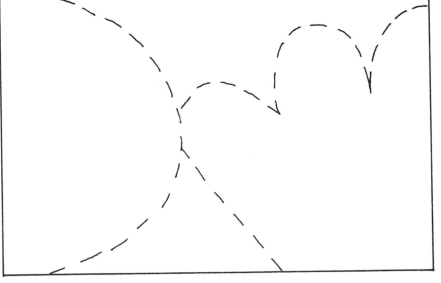

Add lines to separate baskets
from flowers. Add designs as
desired.

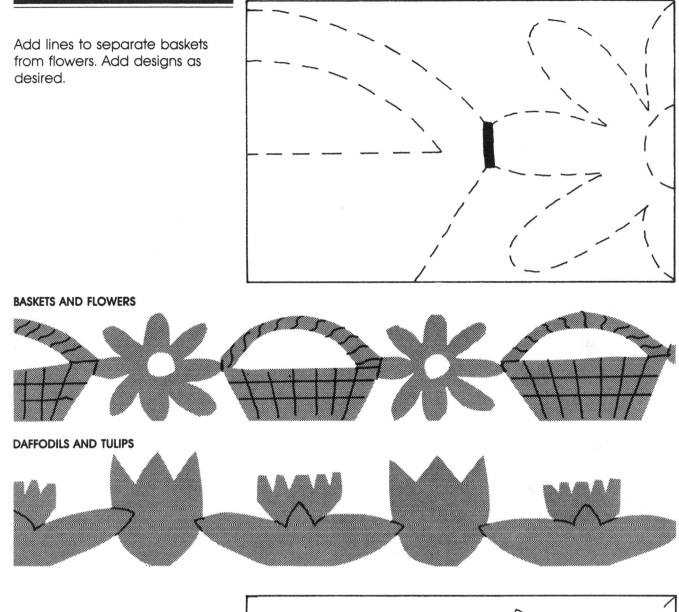

BASKETS AND FLOWERS

DAFFODILS AND TULIPS

Add lines to separate the flowers.

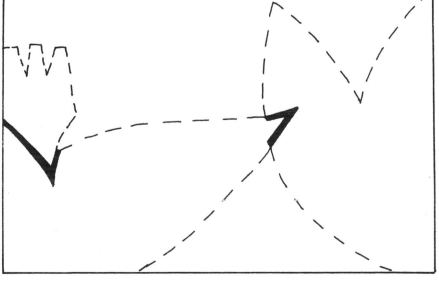

May Figures

May Calendar Keepers

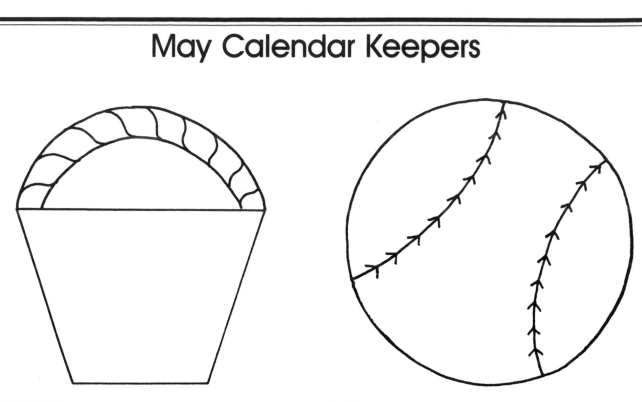

BROWN BASKET

BASEBALL

TULIP

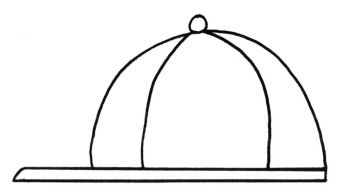

BASEBALL CAP

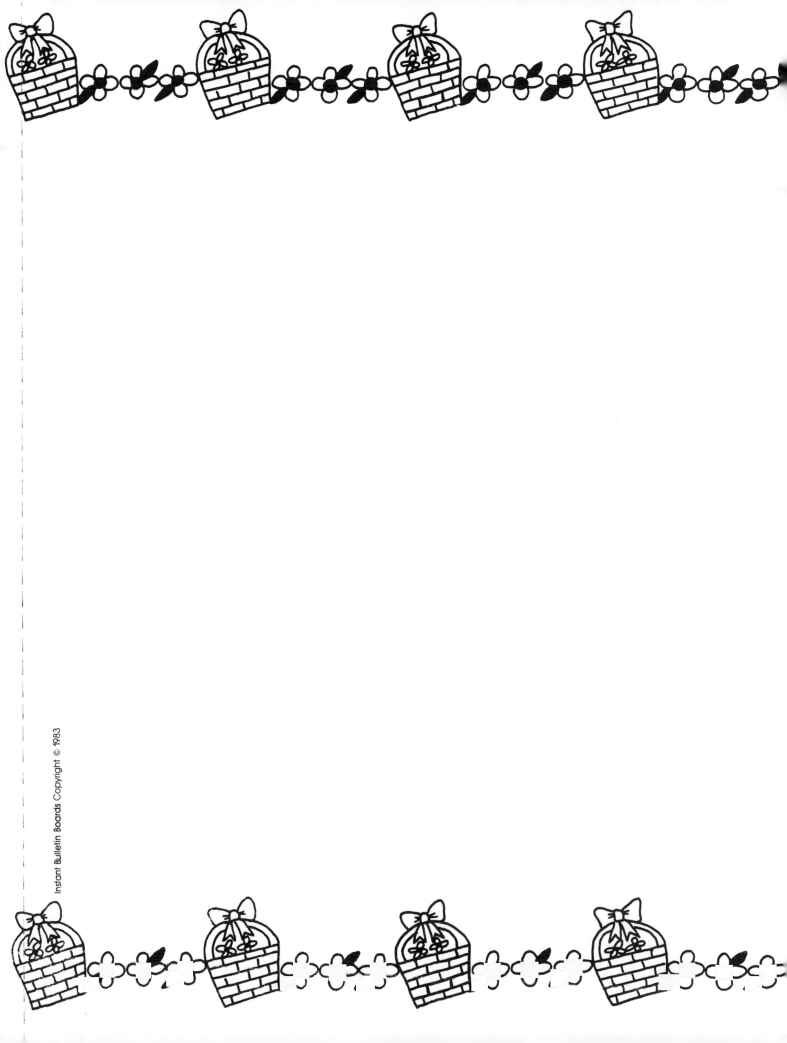

Instant June

June Borders

Add faces to suns. Add lines to separate suns from glasses. Cut out lenses in glasses.

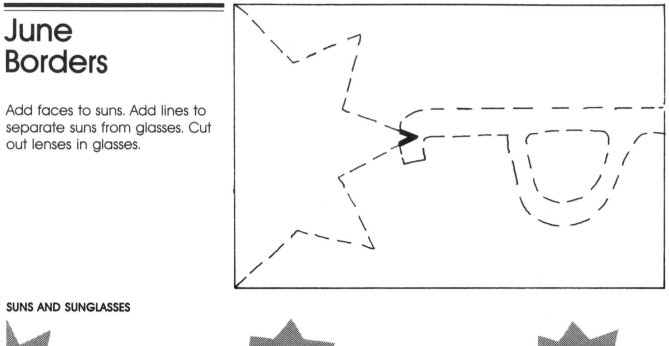

SUNS AND SUNGLASSES

FISH

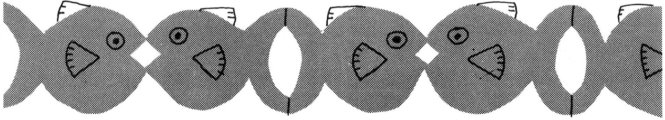

Add eyes and fins to fish. Add cut-out fins to tops of fish.

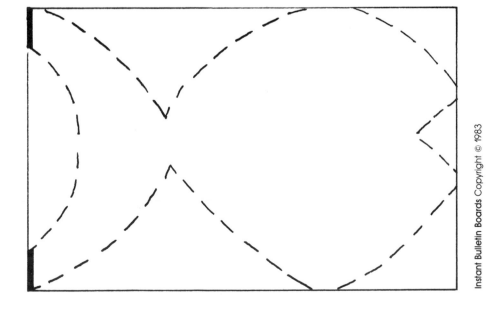

Add lines to separate objects.
Add lines to beachball.

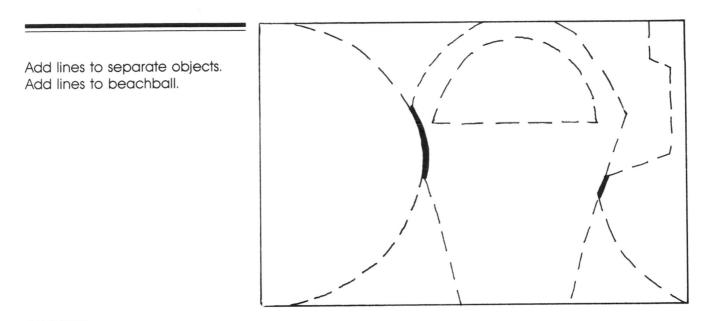

SAND TOYS

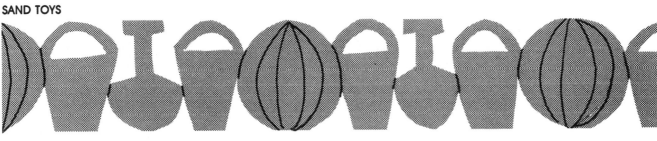

STARFISH AND TREASURE CHESTS

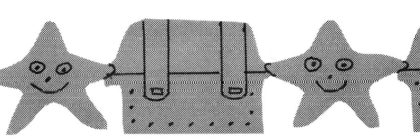
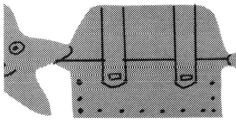

Add faces to starfish. Add lines to treasure chests.

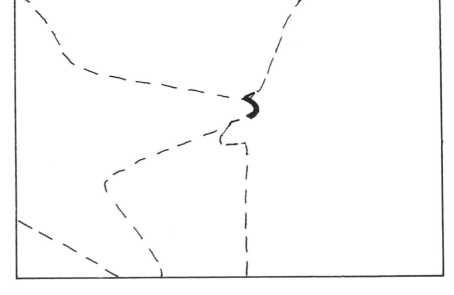

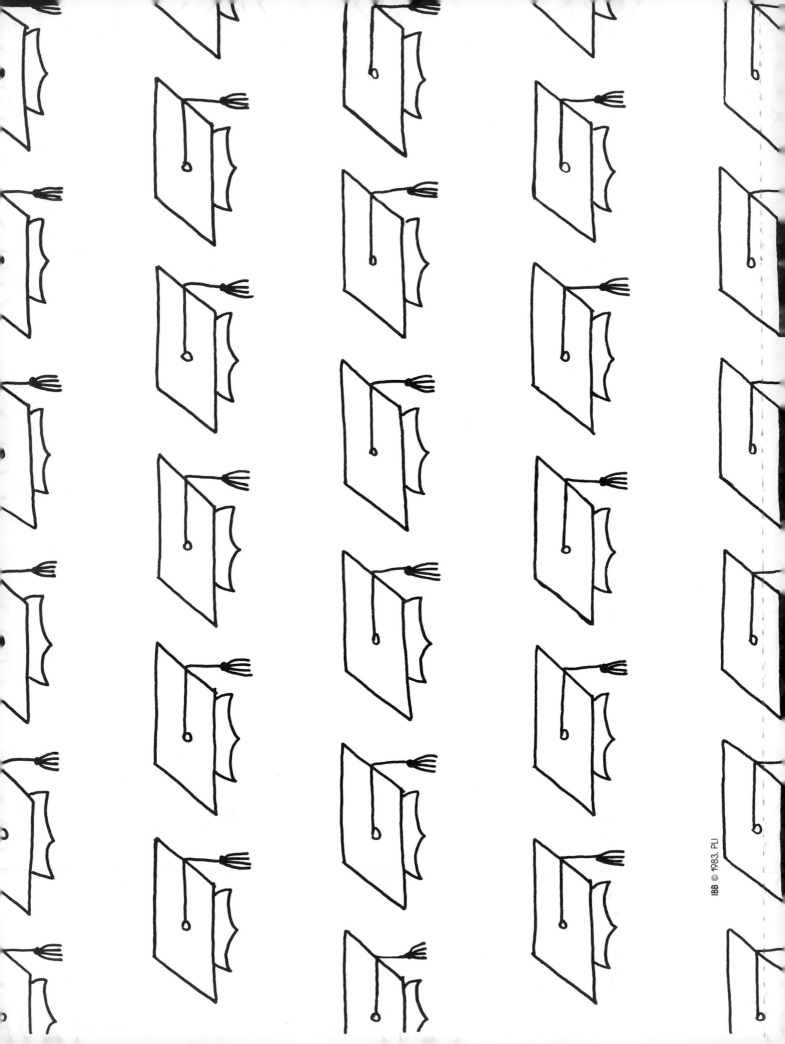

June Figures

June Calendar Keepers

ORANGE SUN

SUNGLASSES

FISH

STARFISH

Letters Appendix

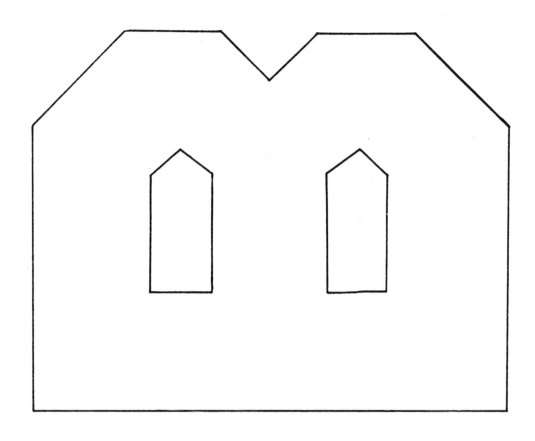

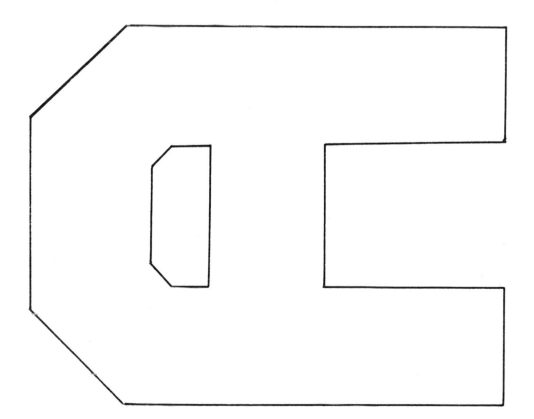

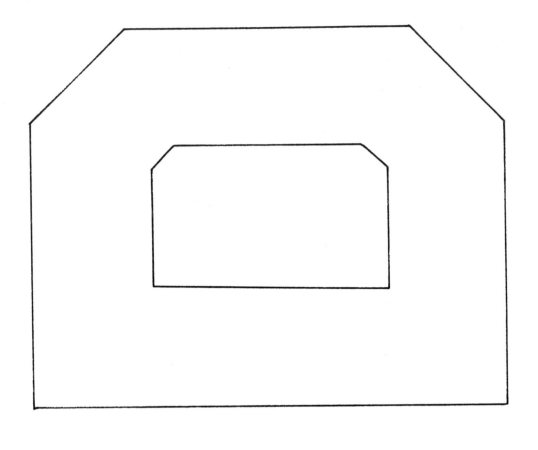

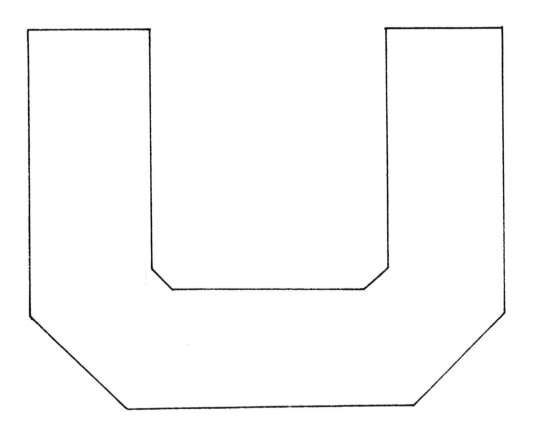

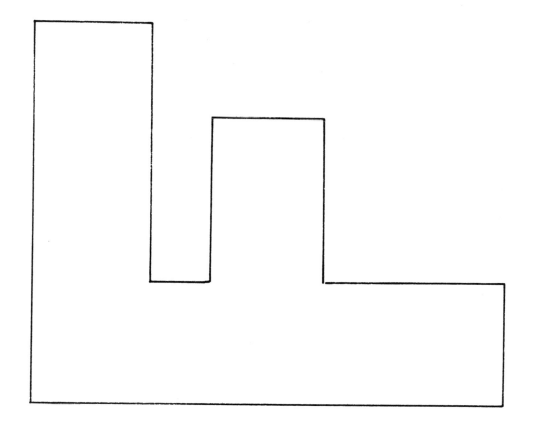

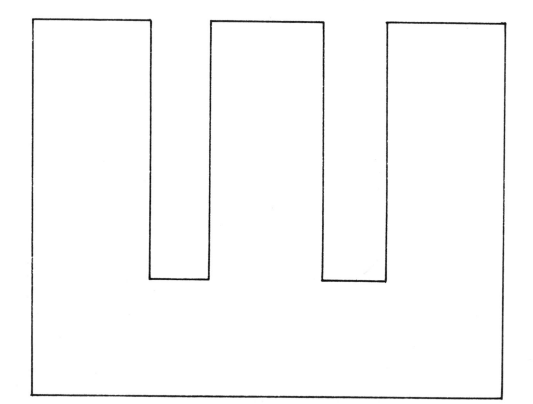

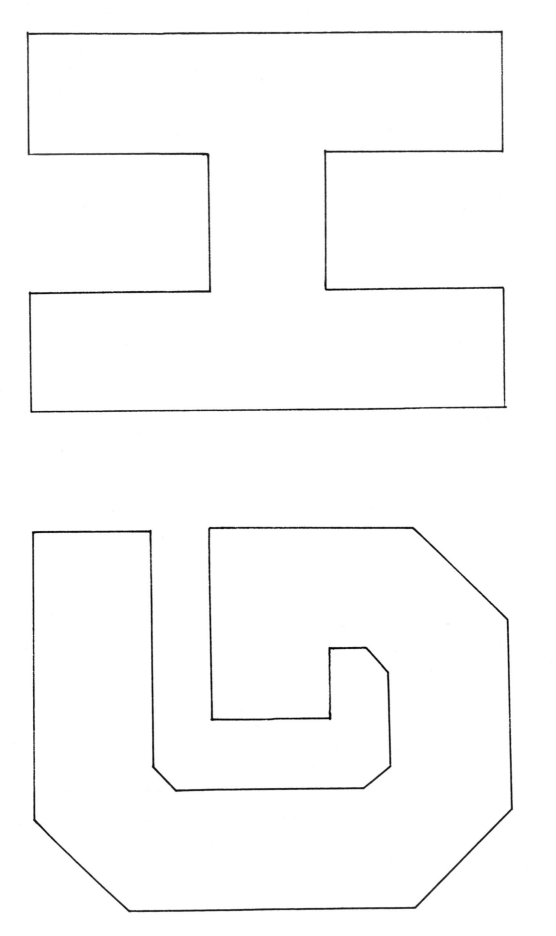

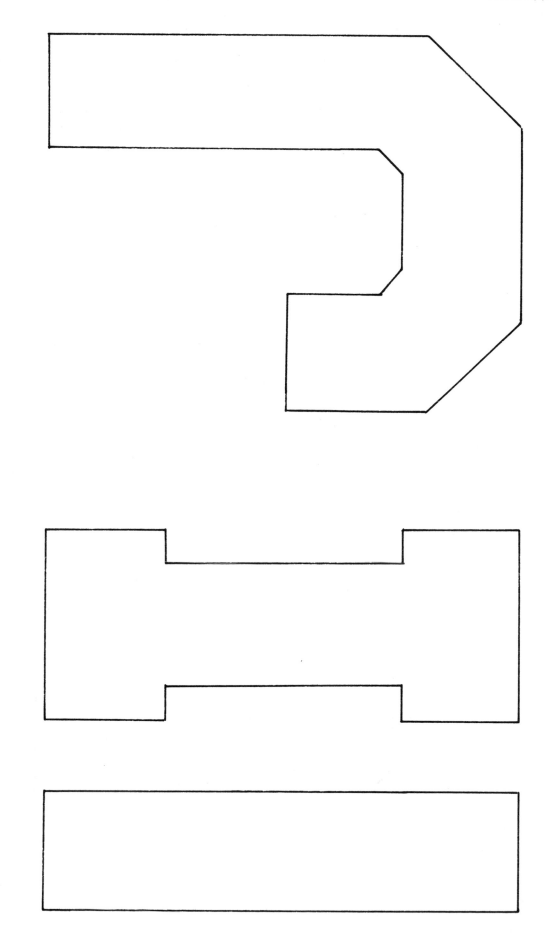

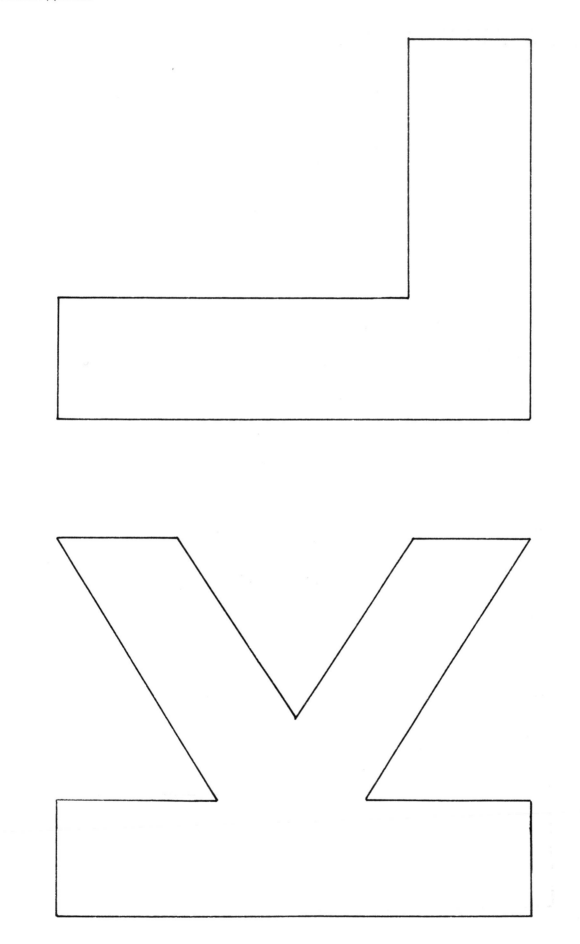

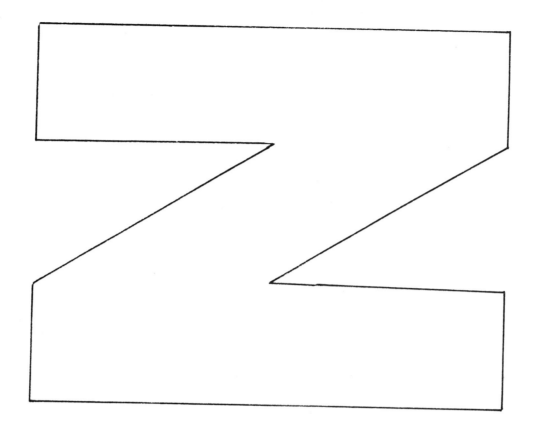

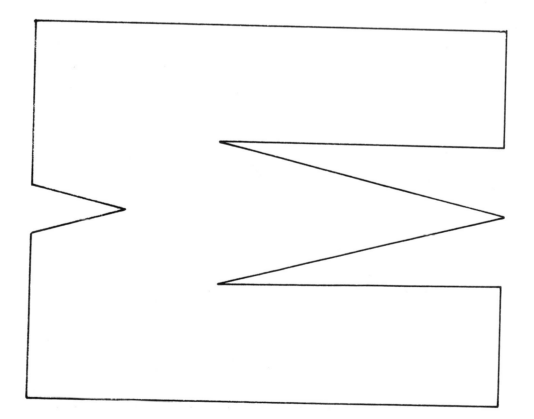

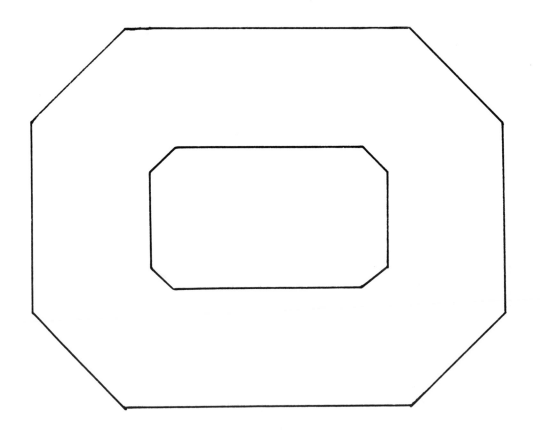

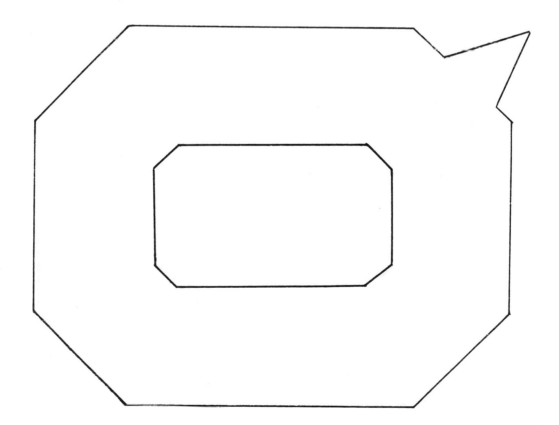

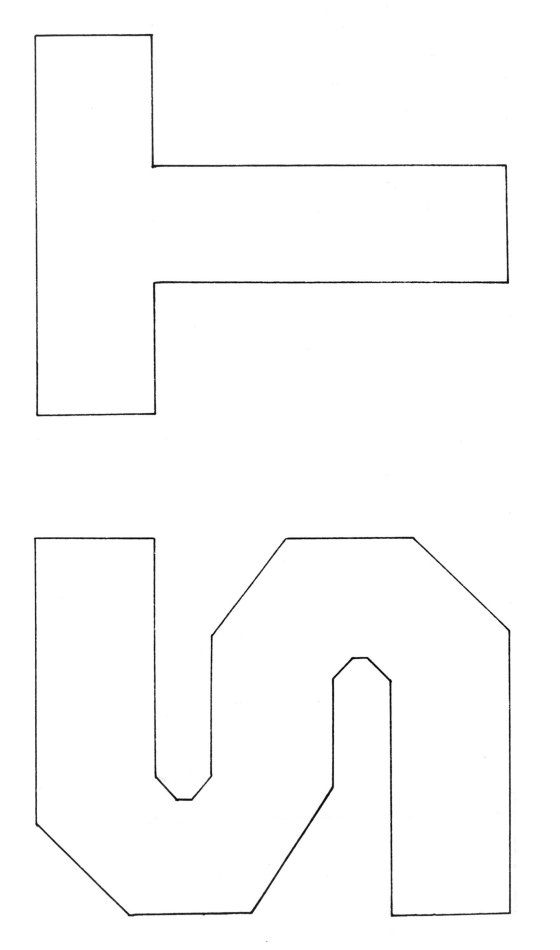

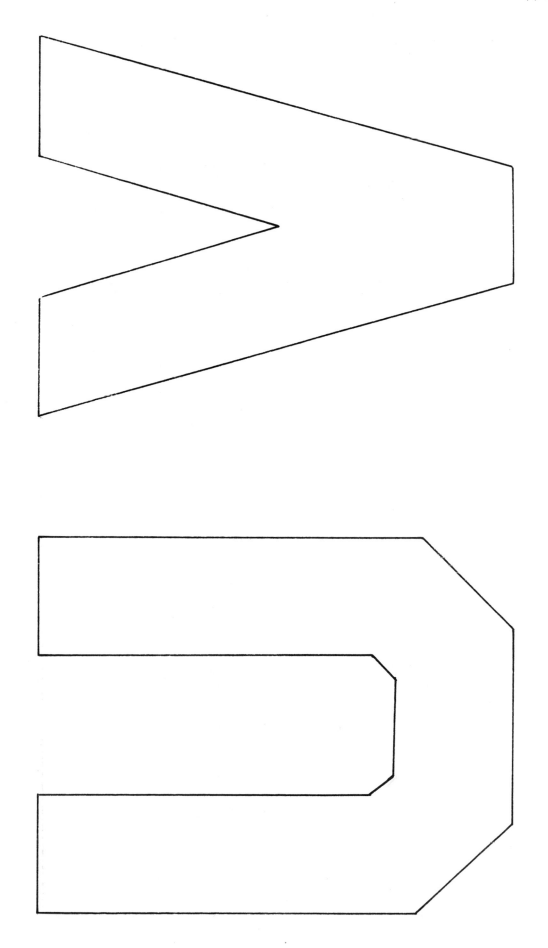

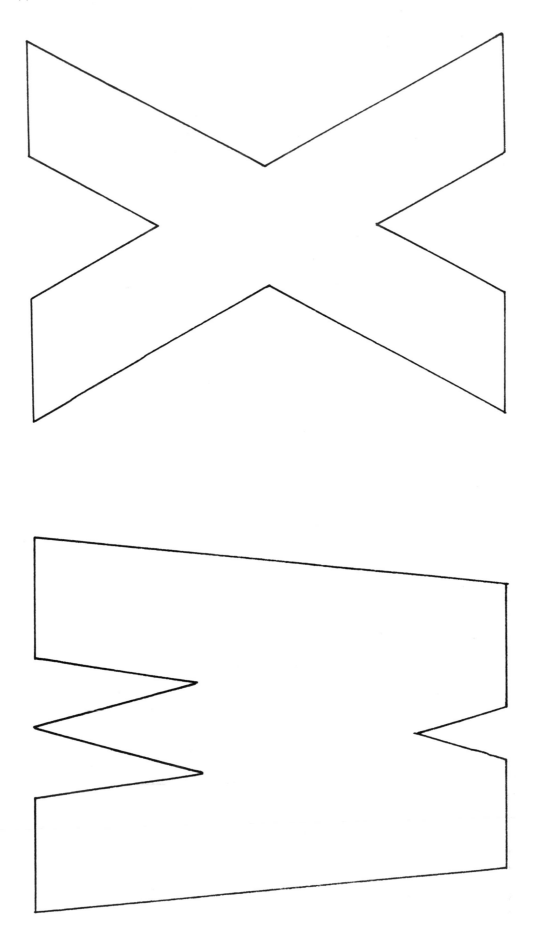

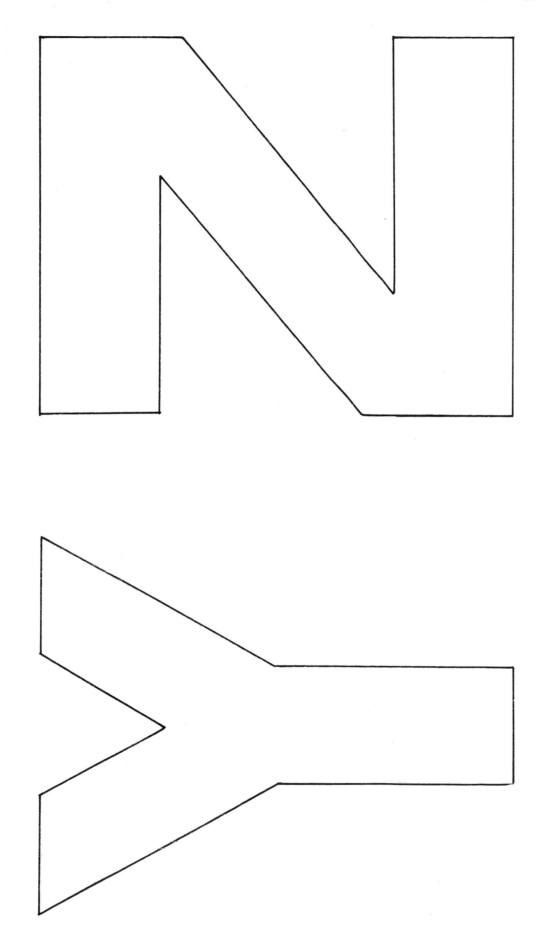

About the Author

Anthony Flores has been teaching a variety of art courses to children and adults since 1963. He has taught for the City of Sacramento Unified School District, the University of California, American River College, and Pepperdine University. In addition to teaching, he has written articles for *Grade Teacher Magazine, Instructor Magazine,* and is the author and illustrator of *Instant Borders.*

Anthony not only teaches, illustrates, and writes, but also plays the guitar and is an excellent gourmet cook. He lives in Sacramento, California, with Muriel, his wife, who is a special education teacher, and his four children, Doug, Chris, Anthony, and Billy.